Leo

of the Tiny Seekers Series

for all the tiny kings and queens of this universe
Aida, especially you

Emily June Ellis

This book belongs to the Tiny Seeker,

____

You are a powerful creator.

Poor Leo and his cold heart felt
fragile and weak.

He didn't feel himself at all.

He was quiet and meek.

He hid from the world,
feeling so broken and frail.

It was as if Leo was under a wicked spell.

It all began when he heard
some bad news.

His heart grew heavy and really confused.

Leo became tired of living with such a
heartbreak.

He just didn't know
how much more he could take.

Leo began searching for purpose
and motivation.

It only took a little *courage* and *action*!

A light within sparkled with comfort
and tickled his pain.

He finally felt happy and alive,
once again!

Leo discovered in a tale of old,
a magical secret that *each* one of us holds.

After stumbling on the most precious wisdom,
warmth and hope finally smothered
Leo's frosty heart.

No matter how brittle or numb,
he knew now that it wasn't too late
to create his fresh start!

THE SECRET
VICTORIA

The legend revealed that a mighty healer and
a powerful wizard exists within us *all*,

and if he or she believed strongly enough,
absolutely **anything** could come true,
BIG or small!

If Leo asked his body and heart to heal and
believed it enough *without* a doubt,

abundance of health and love he then
wouldn't be without!

Leo found that he was in
charge of his own happiness.

His hearty newfound belief
showered him in strength,

shifting his weaknesses to
unspeakable lengths!

His thoughts became his friends
and was very careful
who or what
he chose to fill his *mind.*

Leo picked beautiful things that were
happy, sweet, fun
and *kind.*

He freed himself from all clutter and mess.

Leo had no more sadness or stress!

He saw beauty everywhere and in everything!

It was as if all of nature was in a playful dance.

He felt the wind was humming and singing.

LOVE was in every glance!

Leo finally found the boy he was meant to be!

It was inside him all along just *patiently* waiting to be free!

*This is how Leo discovered the
magic that lives **within**.*

**YOU hold this mighty power too!
You can change anything that
you *truly* believe in!**

The End.

www.ingramcontent.com/pod-product-compliance
Lightning Source LLC
Chambersburg PA
CBHW081301090726
47818CB00080B/210